IMAGES
of America

UXBRIDGE

The depot, shown here on the trackside, was a delightful welcome to railroad passengers as they arrived. Reflected here is the exquisite architecture found throughout Uxbridge.

IMAGES
of America

UXBRIDGE

B. Mae Edwards Wrona

ARCADIA
PUBLISHING

Copyright © 2000 by B. Mae Edwards Wrona
ISBN 978-1-5316-0284-0

Published by Arcadia Publishing
Charleston, South Carolina

Library of Congress Catalog Card Number: 00106444

For all general information contact Arcadia Publishing at:
Telephone 843-853-2070
Fax 843-853-0044
E-mail sales@arcadiapublishing.com
For customer service and orders:
Toll-Free 1-888-313-2665

Visit us on the Internet at www.arcadiapublishing.com

To my two sons, John and Bill.

North Main Street is shown after a snowstorm in the early 1900s. The white house on the right was Horace E. Gunn's home. The only snowplowing in those days was done by the electric cars running up the middle of the road.

CONTENTS

ACKNOWLEDGMENTS

This photographic history of Uxbridge could never have been completed without the help and encouragement of my family and my friend Mary Dolan, whose untiring aid with research and locating pictures was truly appreciated.

Many sources of research materials were used, including early books, town records, Worcester Registry of Deeds records, the *Uxbridge Compendium*, early historical writings, the *Annals of Mendon*, and lastly, information from my own private collection and that of the Uxbridge Historical Society. In particular, I would like to thank Susan Stanovich, librarian of the Uxbridge Public Library, for the use of pictures that have never, until now, been published. Also, my thanks to the library staff for assisting in locating early writings. Thanks go to Jeanette Stanovich, Phyllis Smyth, Shirley Maynard, Edward Gorman, John and Debbie Cnossen, Norma Hoisington, Helen Cairns, Doris Temple, Glen Williams, Joseph Roche, and Raymond and Gladys Courtemanche, all of whom contributed to the hunt for "new" photographs just for this publication.

INTRODUCTION

Uxbridge is located in the beautiful Blackstone Valley, midway between Worcester and Providence, Rhode Island. Since its early years, the gently sloping hills on the west boundary are covered with the fine dwellings of its prosperous citizens, overlooking diversified scenery of meadows, rivers, ponds, and busy workshops. On the east the plains stretch out to the lofty Mendon hillside, whose westerly slopes form the watershed for the West River, which, through the years, furnished the waterpower for the Waucantuck and Elmdale Mills. While gently meandering through the valley, the Blackstone and Mumford Rivers beautify the plains and furnish the power for the numerous other mills that added to the business and prosperity of this enterprising town.

Uxbridge was originally part of Mendon, which, on December 14, 1726, "in answer to our western inhabitants petitioning to be set off as a town or precinct, voted in the negative." However, those western inhabitants became more determined to secede and at a meeting held in Mendon on March 31, 1727, after the reading of the petition of the western inhabitants for a division of the town, the vote was in the affirmative. The western inhabitants lost no time in taking benefit of the vote, for it appears from the records in the Massachusetts Archives, "Towns, Vol. 113, p.714" that the petition and vote was presented to the Massachusetts General Court for its approval and the incorporation of the new town. The act of incorporation passed both houses and became law on June 12, 1727, which is the birthday of the town of Uxbridge.

Farming was the prominent occupation in the beginning, with sawmills and gristmills soon appearing along the rivers, followed by satinet, cotton, and woolen mills, the latter contributing greatly to the prosperity and growth of the town. Churches and schools were built. The Blackstone Canal and the Providence & Worcester Railroad were quick to make an appearance. Fraternal organizations were popular and local groups sponsored baseball and bowling teams. Parades were held and well supported by the townspeople.

The photographs that appear on these pages date from the 1800s through the 1960s and are only a small sample of the life and times of our town, a town that our ancestors were proud to build for the generations that followed. I hope you enjoy this collection of Uxbridge memories.

This aerial view of Williams Hill shows the large farms so typical of early Uxbridge. Seen here are Maple View Farm, on the right, owned for many years by Jacob Wassenar, and Sunnyside Farm, on the left, also known as Hall's Dairy.

One

THE CENTER

The beauty of Uxbridge in its early days shows in this scene at the town center, looking east on Mendon Street in 1875. A.R. Taft's two-story brick building stands on the corner, shaded by the huge elm tree, and the railroad crossing appears on the left.

This photograph, taken in 1875, shows the west side of Main Street. Looking left to right, one sees the Central House, the Phoenix Hardware store, and the Union House, later known as the Whitmore Block.

The first railroad depot was located on what is now called Depot Street. This early photograph shows the depot and, in the background, the engine house. The depot was abandoned when the new station was built in 1895, and an addition to the Bachman Uxbridge Worsted Company covers the tracks.

Hudson's Corner, where a convenience store now sits, had six buildings. The largest building, once known as the Chester House, had 12 rooms on the second and third floors; on the first floor, at one time, Joseph Kelley kept a dry goods store and later, Mr. McShane printed the *Uxbridge Transcript*, a weekly paper there. The other buildings included Hudson's Hardware, a waiting station, a small restaurant, a large storehouse, and a six-compartment octagonal outhouse.

This photograph, looking north from the center and taken before the great fire in 1896, shows the Goldthwaite Block, Phoenix Hardware, the Union House, and the common, on the left. On the right, the Capron's two-story block, Hudson's Corner, and the steeple of the Unitarian church are visible.

Looking south from the common, one can see the Waucantuck House, the Union House, the Goldthwaite Block, and the road rising toward Carpenter's Hill. This photograph was taken before 1896.

Pictured before 1896, the A.R. Taft Block and the Gunn Block included impressive buildings and afforded space for businesses, such as jewelry, clothing, drugs, groceries, millinery, lawyers, a dentist, and the Blackstone National Bank.

After the great fire of 1896, A.R. Taft replaced his two-story wood building with one of brick and added a third floor. On the right can be seen the new H.E. Gunn Building. The watering trough in the center of Mendon Street and the hitching posts along the street were for the convenience of the horse-drawn vehicles.

The old gristmill in the center of town was located on the Mumford River at the dam. The mill was in the rear of the building now owned by Charles Lynch. For many years, the gristmill was operated by John Capron and later by Warren Lackey.

This view of Uxbridge was taken from Capron Hill. Capron Pond in the foreground was once the orchard of Cornet John Farnum, who gave the land to the town so that a dam could be constructed. The many buildings of the Caprons can be seen along the river's edge, and in the far right corner rises the steeple of St. Mary's Church on North Main Street.

The Whitmore Block was one of the first such buildings erected in the center. It was originally called the Union House. In 1862, Harrison and Hannibal Whitmore opened a store here under the name Whitmore Brothers. In 1881, the brothers bought the Union House from Cyrus G. Wood for the sum of $9,500. It was demolished in 1967 to build a parking lot for the Uxbridge Inn.

Horace E. Gunn rebuilt the H.E. Gunn Block after the fire of 1896. Mr. Gunn erected the first building in Uxbridge with plate-glass show windows and modern conveniences. The new building was completed in 1897 and offered, in addition to prescription drugs, a large paint and wallpaper stock "equal to any store in the Blackstone Valley." A full line of cigars, sold by National Cigar Stands, could be had, and the famous line of Rexall Remedies was brought to the store.

On the west side of South Main Street, near the center, is the town hall. This impressive structure was designed by A.P. Cutting of Worcester and was built in 1879. The town lockup was located in the basement. Besides handling the town's business, the town hall was the center of social activities, where traveling stock companies performed, dances were held, and movies were shown. School activities from basketball to graduation exercises, as well as holiday festivities, were all held in the large room on the second floor.

The depot is located on the east side of South Main Street. In May 1893, a bill was presented to the legislature to compel the Providence and Worcester Railroad Company to furnish suitable depot accommodations at Uxbridge. The bill became a law and in July 1894, the new depot was started, stakes being driven into the ground to locate the site. The depot was completed in 1895.

The bank building was sometimes referred to as the Harris Block. On June 15, 1914, the Blackstone National Bank and the Uxbridge Savings Bank opened for business in this new building. Safe-deposit boxes in a fireproof vault were a valuable addition to the services of the Blackstone National Bank. A society called the Improved Order of Red Men held their meetings on the third floor. Over the years, an A&P grocery store, the office of the *Woonsocket Call*, a delicatessen, and a restaurant have been located in this building.

The Daley Brothers General Store was located on Mendon Street near the railroad bridge. Built in the 1800s, the business offered hay, grain, flour, feed, groceries, shoes, fabric for sewing, thread, and other household needs. In the basement was a meat market. In later years, a bowling alley was on the second floor and a barbershop occupied the basement.

This is a very early photograph of the Cornet John Farnum House located on Capron Hill (Mendon Street). Farnum built the house c. 1710, and it was here that the first town meeting was held in 1727. The house still stands today on the same site and is now owned by the Town of Uxbridge and is used as a meeting place for town committees and the Uxbridge Historical Society. It is open to the public the third Sunday of the month from April to October and is thought to be the oldest house in town.

This picture was taken in 1907 and shows the center looking south from the town common. Trolley tracks are visible in the center of the road and hitching posts line the common, with the Hotel Windsor on the south end.

The Hotel Windsor is pictured here in all its beauty. Built in 1881, A.P. Cutting of Worcester was the architect. The first owner, Dr. Levi P. Wilson, named it the Hotel Wilson. The doors of the new hotel were opened on May 20, 1882, with James Barker as proprietor. In March 1883, J.W. and G.F. Day purchased the establishment and changed its name to the Hotel Windsor, a word as similar to the original name as possible to minimize confusion.

At the north end of the common sits the Macomber Academy. At the annual town meeting held on March 3, 1819, voters decided that liberty be given to build a schoolhouse on the town common. Solomon's Temple Lodge of Free Masons and the citizens of the town erected the building by contribution, the citizens building the lower story and the Masons the upper story. The private school, known as Macomber Academy, opened in the fall of 1920. The Masons used the second floor for their meetings.

Soldiers Monument, Uxbridge, Mass.

In the center of the town common stands this monument, a tribute to the soldiers from Uxbridge who fought in the Civil War. The monument was erected by popular subscription in 1898. Dedication exercises were held on September 14, 1898, by the H.H. Legg Post No. 25, Grand Army of the Republic. More than 3,000 people attended. The monument, which faces south, is 19 feet high and cut from Westerly granite. The figure at the top depicts an infantry soldier of 1861–1865 at parade rest. The cost of the monument was approximately $4,000.

In this picture of the common looking east, one can see the Civil War monument, the Thayer Memorial Library, and the Unitarian church. The hitching posts still line the common.

The Thayer Memorial Library is located on the east side of North Main Street, next to the Unitarian church. On February 20, 1893, Edwin C. Thayer of Keene, New Hampshire, addressed the Uxbridge Board of Selectmen, proposing to erect a building to cost not less than $20,000 to be used as a free public library. The library was to be built in memory of his mother and father near the Unitarian church. Thayer's proposition was unanimously accepted at the town meeting held on March 18, 1893. The building was designed and built by Fuller & Delano, Architects, of Worcester at a total cost of $33,500, including furniture. Dedication ceremonies were held on June 20, 1894.

Constructed in 1914, the building that held the Uxbridge Savings Bank and the Blackstone National Bank was extensively rebuilt between 1939 and 1955. The Blackstone Bank was Uxbridge's first bank. In 1865, it was reincorporated as the Blackstone National Bank. Moses Taft founded the Uxbridge Savings Bank in 1870. Previously, the banks were housed in the Bank Building on South Main Street.

The Jefferson House on North Main Street is believed to have been built by Simeon Wheelock, a blacksmith from Mendon, in 1768 or 1769. Shortly before his death, Wheelock sold this house to Royal Jefferson, a blacksmith, who in the early 19th century built a new blacksmith shop on the site of the present Unibank. At one time the house was rented to Elihu Brown. In the early 20th century, William E. Hayward purchased the house and, in 1910, he and his wife donated it to the Deborah Wheelock Chapter of the Daughters of the American Revolution.

Erected in 1921, the World War I monument was placed on the north end of the common. The monument is made of marble that is technically known as Italian statuary marble. On the sides of the tablet are bronze representations of the implements of warfare actually used in WW I. A bronze American eagle perches atop the tablet, its feet clutching a marble globe, which rests on a marble replica of three-inch shells.

In front of the WW I monument sits this 105mm (4.7-inch) Knapp German rifle, captured by the 77th Division in the Meuse-Argonne in October 1918. The Charles A. Rice Post No. 33, American Legion, presented the rifle to the Town of Uxbridge on November 11, 1933.

When the Taft brothers rebuilt their block after the 1896 fire, they added a third floor, which was occupied by the Uxbridge Lodge, IOOF. Taft Brothers Grocery occupied the first floor. On the street is the ten-bench open car of the Milford and Uxbridge Street Railway.

This is a view of Main Street looking south from the common in early 1906. All of the buildings destroyed in the 1896 fire had been replaced by this time.

The H.E. Gunn Block, pictured in 1907, has a new painted sign on the north wall. At the time maple trees lined South Main Street.

Looking north from Main Street in 1907, the street is lined with beautiful maple trees and the Milford and Uxbridge trolley is approaching the center.

This picture of Main Street looking south shows the changes that continually took place as Uxbridge grew. The Vernon Drug Company has opened in the old Taft Brothers store, an addition has been made to the H.E. Gunn Block, and automobiles have replaced horse-drawn carriages.

25

This street scene of the center, taken in the 1940s, shows some further changes that have taken place. The Boston Store is located in the Farnum Block, the First National Store is in the Chester House Building, and the Worcester Suburban Electric Company has an office in the Taft Building. The marque for the Cameo Theater, located in the Mechanic Square area in back of the Farnum Block, advertises Dana Andrews and Gene Tierney in *Where the Sidewalk Ends* and *Trail of the Yukon*.

After the 1938 hurricane destroyed the tower of the town hall, major improvements were made to the building. A two-floor addition was built on the north side. The tower, however, was not rebuilt. At about the same time, a new fire station was built on the south side.

At the March 2, 1885 town meeting, voters authorized a village or district in the northern end of Uxbridge containing not less than 1,000 inhabitants. The village was called North Uxbridge, and this is a view of Main Street.

The old Spring Tavern located on West Hartford Avenue was known for its excellent purl and flip. Purl was a medicated or spiced malt liquor, and flip was a hot drink containing beer, cider, or the like, with sugar, egg, and spice, usually nutmeg.

In 1903, the town built this fire station on Main Street in North Uxbridge at a cost of $2,403. Men of the North Uxbridge Fire Department pose with the equipment. They are, from left to right, as follows: (front row) Edward Wilson, Clarence Hawley, Marcus Carter, Richard Pearson, Samuel Moore, Frank J. Mills, Dr. George T. Little, George Wilmot, Rev. Adonirum Hopkins, Edward Stansfield, William White, and Arnold S. Allen, fire chief; (middle row) Charles Gifford, George H. Ashton, and driver Joseph Buckley; (back row) James Bryant, Charles Johnson, Charles F. Britton, Peter Rainville, William Malley, and Albert A. Sherman.

Two

RIVERS AND BRIDGES

Taken in 1909, this photograph shows the stone arch bridge on East Hartford Avenue in North Uxbridge that spans the Mumford River near the Crown and Eagle Mills.

This historic log dam was built across the Mumford River in the center of town near Lynch's. For many years Henry Capron operated a sawmill on the east side of the river, and on the west side was the old gristmill. A masonry dam replaced the log dam in 1910.

When the new masonry dam was built to replace this old log dam, a plank walk 2 feet wide extended clear across the dam, allowing repairs to be made on the flashboards.

Visible beyond the log dam on the west side of the Mumford River are the gristmill and other buildings on the Capron property. These buildings have all been demolished over the years.

A dam was built on the Mumford River in North Uxbridge to furnish power for the Clapp Mill. The dam was often referred to as "the falls," and the body of water behind the dam was called Mumford Pond.

The West River originates in the town of Upton. Although it runs through the easterly part of Uxbridge, it retains the name West River, given when it was the western boundary of Mendon.

This scene on the West River shows the dam that was built near the Waucantuck Mill, with the trolley bridge in the background. This was the track used by the Uxbridge and Milford trolley line.

The Blackstone River has its source in North Pond in Worcester. In its course through Worcester, Millbury, Sutton, Grafton, Northbridge, and Uxbridge, the river receives the waters of several tributary streams; its constantly increasing size and volume furnishes, by the time it reaches Uxbridge, a seldom-failing power. It was this power that gave to the town its great prosperity as a manufacturing center.

On the Blackstone River in the Rice City section, a dam and a stone arch bridge were built. The Blackstone Canal had locks nearby this dam.

This bridge served carriages, automobiles, and people where the Blackstone River passes by the Stanley Woolen Mill on Mendon Street.

As an alternative way to cross the river, this trolley bridge was built a short distance south of the road bridge.

When the petition was granted to build a new depot, railroad officials brought up the matter of grade crossings needed to move the tracks. The work was accomplished by raising the tracks, building a bridge over Mendon Street, and lowering the road. In the process, the beauty of the old John Capron Homestead was diminished, as the front entrance faced the granite wall necessary for raising the tracks.

This photograph shows the top of the bridge with one set of rails completed—the second set to follow. In the background can be seen the gambrel roof of the lovely John Capron Homestead, its beauty impaired by the new construction.

This dam, built across the Blackstone River, was taken down after spring floods in 1926 threatened to break it and cause extensive damage in Uxbridge, Millville, Blackstone, and Woonsocket. The dam was located on the south side of Mendon Street near the Stanley Woolen Mill.

Three

HOMES AND FAMILIES

Brookside Farm was owned and operated by George Farnum, a descendent of Cornet John Farnum. George Farnum dealt in butter, pure cream, eggs, and chickens. His farm was located on Ironstone Road, now called Quaker Highway.

The Willard Judson Homestead on Pleasant Street sits on a hill overlooking the center of town. The "town clock" in the steeple of the Unitarian church was his gift to the town. It was not until after his death, however, that the people were told the donor's name. The Judson Homestead passed from Willard Judson to Abbie Taft and in recent years has been owned by Arthur Wheelock.

Deacon William Capron built this house on North Main Street c. 1821. After 1875, the house was known locally as the Henry Capron Home. Henry Capron briefly operated a gristmill at Uxbridge Center. He was active in public affairs, serving as town clerk and treasurer from 1875–1876, a trustee of the Uxbridge Savings Bank, and a trustee of the Uxbridge Public Library. In later years the house was owned by Ernest Picard and his wife and, today, it is the home of Cove Insurance.

Although known as the Robert Taft House, this home on the west side of the town common may have been built for Effingham Capron or his brother. Robert Taft, a merchant and manufacturer, bought the house prior to 1866. He was one of the owners of the Taft Brothers Grocery and of a hay and grain business located on Depot Street.

John Capron purchased this house from Seth Read in 1790. The home is one of five gambrel-roofed houses in Uxbridge. The ell of the house was once used as an inn; later it was kept as a cobbler shop. The main house had walls that were elaborately stenciled, and it was considered a "real showplace," with terraced gardens stretching up to the main road. All this beauty was diminished when the railroad tracks were raised and the overhead bridge was built in 1895. In later years, an addition was attached to the Mendon Street side of the house where paint store, barber shop, and grocery businesses were located.

Built c. 1874, the Charles C. Capron House is Uxbridge's finest example of Victorian Gothic-style residential architecture. Charles Capron was a local manufacturer and a third-generation member of the locally prominent Capron family. Together with his cousin Henry Capron, Charles Capron began his manufacturing career in the Capron Mill, built by his father in 1820. He served the town in several public offices and was representative to the Massachusetts General Court.

This view of Capron Street, lined with large elm trees, was taken in 1906.

The Israel Southwick House sits on the corner of Mendon and Oak Streets. In 1893, Southwick and his brother-in-law Richard Sayles rented the newly built Central Woolen Mill from Moses Taft. They sold their lease to Bradford Taft & Company c. 1861. Through the years, the house has been remodeled several times, but the barn remains in its original condition.

The Deacon William Lackey House is located on the east corner of Oak and Mendon Streets. Lackey was a flour and grain dealer and for some time ran the Capron Gristmill on the Mumford River. Lackey and his heirs continued to own the house throughout the last half of the 19th century. Other owners have been Louis Maroney and Charles Lynch.

The Henry Ellison House is located on Oak Street near East Hartford Avenue. Henry A. Ellison owned the farm from 1855 to 1870, when it passed to Henry M. Ellison. Both Ellisons operated the property as a farm. In later years John Voss purchased the property and named it River Bend Farm. The farm is now part of the Blackstone River Valley Heritage Corridor and the barn is the Visitor's Center.

Richard Sayles, the owner of this impressive stone house located on Mendon Street, was for many years associated with the Rivulet Mill in North Uxbridge. Together with his brother-in-law Israel Southwick, the mill was enlarged and steam power installed in 1865. Sayles died in 1887, and his three sons ran the mill until 1910. The house still stands today, but the barn in the rear has been converted to apartments.

The Albert A. Sprague House on Mendon Street is a well-preserved Queen Anne-style design. Sprague was a bookkeeper, who during the early 20th century worked for C.A. Root Company as a clerk. He also held several local public offices, including trustee of the public library.

The Jacob Taft Homestead has a long history of owners. Jacob Taft acquired the property in 1880 from Henry Spencer and owned the home until 1893, when it was transferred to Anna Wood. Wood deeded the property to Marcia Griswald in 1909. The next transfer recorded was to Thomas and Theresa Kennedy from Eva O. Farnum in 1923. In 1969, the house was deeded from the Kennedys to Sandra Lemire. The house is still standing, although some exterior changes have been made.

Dr. A.E. Gray, D.D.S., originally had offices in the Taft Building in the center of town and was one of the tenants at the time of the 1896 fire. Gray lost most of his belongings in the two rooms nearest to Gunn's Block. Subsequently, he moved his office to this home. His son Homer Gray studied dentistry and then joined his father in the business.

This large brick house was located on Capenter's Hill (South Main Street). It was believed to have been a Carpenter residence. During the early 1900s, it was converted to apartments and later was demolished to make way for three small houses built on the same lot.

An interesting example of Federalist design with Victorian decorative details is found in this cottage owned by Josiah Cummings in 1855. Located on High Street, the cottage faces Pleasant Street. Other owners have been Louis Murdock (1870), F. Goldthwaite (1898), and station agent William Perkins (early 1900s).

Joseph Taft built this home on the west side of South Main Street. He was a farmer who owned significant acreage around the house. In the 19th century, the property passed to Zadock Taft and then to his son George Z. Taft. In the 1930s, the barn and pasture were used by C.A. Root for some of his Elmwood Farm herd. On the north side of the house, Root built an ice cream stand, called the Chalet. The building is now used by a real estate agency.

In 1807, Bezaleel Taft built this house and small brick building for his son Bezaleel Taft Jr., who had graduated from Harvard College in 1804 and was admitted to the bar c. 1807. When Bezaleel Taft Jr. died, the house went to his son Henry Gordon Taft and then, in turn, to his son George S. Taft, a lawyer. All three Tafts practiced law in Uxbridge and in law firms in Worcester and Boston.

The Honorable Bezaleel Taft built this house in 1780 or earlier. In addition to being one of the most sophisticated Georgian-style homes in southern Worcester County, the house has been associated with six generations of the locally prominent Taft family. The farm on which the house stands had been owned since the early 18th century by Daniel Taft and his son Josiah Taft, both of whom were among the wealthiest citizens of Uxbridge. Bezaleel Taft's mother, Josiah Taft's widow, was allowed to vote on the matter of special taxes sought to support the colonies, the only woman allowed to do so locally before the 20th century.

This photograph, looking east on Douglas Street, shows Abell's Creamery and the strawberry gardens of Charles Talbot. In the far center can be seen the old St. Mary's Church on North Main Street, and to the right are the spires of the Unitarian and Congregational churches.

This view of Douglas Street in the early years of Uxbridge shows the home of Dr. Leonard White and, in the background, the buildings and barns along North Main Street. Snowling Road, a street connecting North Main and Douglas Streets, was laid out on the west side of this property.

Charles Talbot built his home on the north side of Douglas Street, looking east towards the center of town. Talbot had an extensive garden on his property. He came to Uxbridge in 1861 and, after working ten years in Center Mill, he took up farming in Rice City, devoting special attention to the raising of fruit and vegetables, with strawberries a specialty. In 1899, he moved his business to Douglas Street, where he originated the Talbot Strawberry.

This view shows more of Charles Talbot's gardens and fruit trees.

The William E. Hayward House, an outstanding mid-Victorian design, is located on the east side of North Main Street. William Hayward was a local banker and industrialist. During the 1860s and 1870s, he was a partner in the firm of Capron and Hayward, manufacturing satinets at the Capron Mill on Mendon Street. After 1870, he was a trustee of the Uxbridge Savings Bank and president of the Blackstone National Bank in 1893.

The Lackey House on North Main Street was built c. 1880. Mr. Lackey was a carpenter and builder. The house was trimmed with gingerbread, a popular decoration in those years.

Eugene Lackey built this house on North Main Street in 1907. He was a housepainter and wallpaper hanger.

John Taft, a farmer and lumber dealer, lived here during much of the 19th century. Taft had a small millpond and sawmill, which existed between 1830 and 1870. Probably built c. 1749, the house is one of only five gambrel-roofed cottages built in the town during the 18th century. The house is frequently referred to as the Aaron Taft House.

This picture of Charles Seagrave's house was taken in 1911. From 1870 to 1875, Seagrave carried on a hardware and furniture store alongside his undertaking business, in the building on Mendon Street near the railroad bridge. He sold the store in 1875, retaining his undertaking business until 1895, when he passed it on to his son Augustus C. Seagrave. For several years, Charles Seagrave served as coroner and overseer of the poor. He also served as a selectman for 20 years and as a state representative in 1880.

The Stowe Tavern, also known as Wood's Tavern, was located in Rice City at the five corners. It is said that George Washington drove into the yard and was served refreshments by Mrs. Stowe. A 1798 almanac says, "the Probate Court of Worcester County will be held the fourth Tuesday in May and November at the house of Mr. Wood, inn-holder in Uxbridge." Over the years this house fell into disrepair; destroyed by fire, it was never rebuilt.

The James Whitin Estate was on the south side of East Hartford Avenue. It was a large home with an indoor swimming pool and all the modern conveniences of the time. Whitin also kept a string of polo ponies and hosted polo matches on the grounds of the estate. After the death of Mrs. Whitin, the estate was sold and became a treatment center for alcoholics. It was destroyed by fire in 1991.

The James Whitin Estate had its own water supply stored in this water tower built on the highest point on the property.

This stable, built on the east side of the James Whitin Estate, included not only an accommodation for his polo ponies but also a bowling alley and other recreational facilities. In the photograph below, the windows of the horse stables can be seen.

The M. Aldrich House on West Street was originally a saltbox style home. During the 19th century, it was heavily altered and, therefore, no longer looks like this. M. Aldrich owned the farm in 1855, and A. Aldrich owned it from 1857 to 1870. This is one of several farms in South Uxbridge belonging to members of the Aldrich family, many of whom were Quakers. Helen Cairns currently owns the house.

The M. Aldrich barn was built on the west side of the street. Destroyed in the 1938 hurricane, it was never rebuilt.

Four

MILLS AND BUSINESSES

This is one of Taft Brothers delivery wagons. The side panel advertises Pillsbury's Best products.

The Aldrich sawmill was built c. 1830, probably by Daniel Aldrich, a wheelwright. In the industrial census of 1850, Aldrich is listed as employing three men to produce wagons, shingles, lumber, and boards, using hand labor and waterpower. After Aldrich's death, the mill became the property of his son Gideon Aldrich. The mill, located on Aldrich Street, has in recent years fallen into disrepair and is no longer visible.

The Ironstone Factory was built in 1815 in the area called Ironstone in the southeastern part of town. It burned in 1832 and was rebuilt. Again in 1865, it burned; this time the mill was not rebuilt, but a roof was installed over the remaining basement walls. It was used as a shoddy mill in 1879. In 1900, when the Ironstone Schoolhouse burned, temporary classrooms were set up here for the children of Ironstone Village.

The Standard Laundry, operated by a Mr. MacKenzie, was located on Maple Street in North Uxbridge. It was the first steam laundry business in town.

Joshua Garside ran a boot shop in this building on Henry Street, opposite the Wheelocksville School, c. 1850. The Sessions family owned the building for more than a century. Three families lived in the former boot shop until 1954, when the building was leveled.

The Waucantuck Mill was originally built by Luke Taft in 1834. It burned in 1837 and was rebuilt in 1838. In 1846, C.A. and S.M. Wheelock owned and operated it under the name of the Waucantuck Mill, from the Indian name, Waruntug. In 1900, Charles A. Root and Louis Bachman formed their business here. In 1905, William J. Brady bought the mill and operated it until 1961.

This winter scene of Hecla Village shows the Hecla Mill in the foreground. The American Woolen Company owned this mill at one time.

In 1810, Daniel Day built a mill on this site. The mill burned in 1844 and was rebuilt a year or two later. In 1852, Samuel Scott leased the mill and manufactured satinets. He was so successful that he bought the mill and farm from Day in 1859. The business became the firm of J.R. Scott and Company. Although no longer in operation, the mill still stands today.

Granite quarries were an active business in Uxbridge. Much granite was shipped from this town to build bridges, foundations, and other structures. The granite was much sought after by large construction companies in Providence, New Bedford, and New York. This quarry was owned and operated by the Blanchard brothers.

The Rivulet Mill was built in 1814. It was idle for several years before Richard Sayles bought it from Deacon Chandler Taft. The mill was enlarged and steam power installed in 1865. Sayles remained in the business until his death in 1857, when his three sons took over. In 1923, the Uxbridge Worsted bought the mill and owned it until 1960, when it was sold to the Nelmore Corporation of Millville.

Robert Rogerson of Taunton built the Crown and Eagle Mills, located on East Hartford Avenue in North Uxbridge. The mill with the belfry was built between 1825 and 1827 and was called the Crown in honor of England, the birthplace of Rogerson's parents. The other mill was built between 1830 and 1832 and was called the Eagle in honor of America, the parents' foster home. Both mills burned in 1976.

This view, looking east towards the center of town, shows Shuttle Shop Pond, the old fire engine house, and the shuttle shop. On the right is Arthur Taft's large barn, now an apartment building. For years the Tafts cut ice from the pond until the water became contaminated and they were forced to move their ice business to North Uxbridge.

Charles Hudson stands in front of his store in the center on Mendon Street. This corner was also called Hudson's Corner. Before the center school was built, the town rented space on the second floor of this building to use as a high school.

George C. Abells manufactured ice cream at the Blackstone Valley Creamery building in the center of Uxbridge from 1894 to 1900. After that he moved to his own plant on Douglas Street. Abells did both wholesale and retail business from this building.

In April 1905, the Calumet and Hecla Mills were sold at auction. Arthur Wheelock purchased the Calumet and renamed the mill the Stanley Woolen Company. This picture shows the mill as it looked in 1907. The mill remained in the Wheelock family until it closed.

Workers at the Stanley Woolen Company pause for picture taking during their lunch period. This picture was taken in the early 1900s.

James Daley owned a grocery business in this house, located at Hecla and Mendon Streets. This area was called Daley's Corner. Along with groceries Daley sold ice cream, candy, and hay, and he had a livery stable in the rear of the building. Daley's was a favorite gathering place for the men who lived in the area.

Frank J. Mills's bakery was located on West Hartford Avenue near Elm Street in North Uxbridge. Frank Mills also did catering for weddings, parties, and other occasions.

Maurice Lofstedt, second from the left, takes his friends out for a ride in his 1911 International pickup truck. Lofstedt owned and operated an electrical business at the corner of Douglas Street and Snowling Road. With Lofstedt are, from left to right, Alfred Demers, "Cracksy" Vincent, and Earle Vincent.

This very early truck was, perhaps, the beginning of Emmott Valley Transportation. It was equipped with solid rubber tires. Pictured, from left to right, are Edward Emmott, owner; Neil Fraetus, helper; and William Borden, driver.

This truck was owned by the Waucantuck Mills. The driver could not be identified.

Some of the workers in a local textile mill take time out from lunch to have their picture taken. Neither the location nor the workers could be identified.

This is the interior of the Daley Brothers Store on Mendon Street near the railroad bridge.

This is the interior of the Taft Brothers Grocery Store, with Robert Taft and his son at the counter. The store was located in the Taft Block on the corner of Main and Mendon Streets.

The Taft Brothers Store was for years the town's largest grocery. In the picture reading left to right are: John Carmody, Fred Taft, Sadie MacNeil, Tom Baker, Ray Holland, Everett Southwick, and William Waterhouse.

This interior view of the Taft Brothers Store, with all the employees standing in the center, shows the large variety of products available at the time.

The interior of H. E. Gunn's drugstore in 1908 shows the unique soda counter and well-stocked shelves that Gunn so proudly advertised.

The A&P store, located in the Bank Building on South Main Street, was equipped with all the modern conveniences of the early 1900s. Standing at the counter ready to serve customers are Joseph Bertrand and John Cnossen.

John Gorman owned and operated a bakery in North Uxbridge. This 1922 photograph shows him delivering bread in a horse-drawn sleigh. The sleigh guaranteed that weather was never a problem.

As years went by, John Gorman continued his bread deliveries. Although his services never changed, his equipment did—as can be seen in this view of him with his new delivery wagon in the 1930s.

One of the town's enterprising businesses began in this small building on North Main Street. In 1923, Nicholas Frabotta opened a gasoline station at this location, a short distance south of his father's station.

As the business grew, so did the station. Nicholas Frabotta put an addition on the south side and, soon after, he found it necessary to put an addition on the north side. As his business continued to expand, he added fuel storage tanks and a fleet of large oil tankers. The station is still doing business at this site but is now owned by Edward Bedard.

Two open trolleys are parked in the Worcester Street Railway Carhouse on North Main Street. When the streetcars were replaced with buses, this garage continued to serve as an operations center.

Trolley No. 812 was a closed car that serviced the town. The Worcester Consolidated Street Railway built the carhouse in 1901 and furnished trolley service to North Uxbridge, Uxbridge, Millville, Blackstone, and Woonsocket, Rhode Island. The last year of operation was 1927.

George Corbeille's Texaco service station was located on the east side of South Main Street next to the depot. It was equipped with an outside car lift and the latest model gas pumps.

Felix Frabotta owned this gas station located on Main Street in North Uxbridge. Vincenzo and Antoinette Frabotta operated the grocery and liquor store on the north side of the building. The buses in the picture were driven by Vincenzo and Nicholas Frabotta and furnished transportation for mill workers throughout the town.

The Moxie Company's sales promotion car stops at Blaine's Variety store on the corner of Court and Douglas Streets in the late 1930s. The driver was a man dressed in a riding habit, and the driver's seat was the saddle of the large white horse.

Looking west on Rivulet Street in this 1930 photograph, the Rivulet Mill can be seen on the left and the mill office on the right. In the center of the picture is the mill tenement house.

Nicholas Frabotta and his two sons, Nicholas O. and Felix C. Frabotta donated the first ambulance in the town's history in 1954.

The New England Power Company was located on Depot Street.

The Taft Brothers hay and grain business on Depot Street served area farmers for many years.

The Uxbridge Public Market, Joe's Barber Shop, and Creighton's Paint Store (formerly Carter's) conducted business in the old Capron House on Mendon Street. The building was demolished in 1967 to make a parking lot for Lynch Pharmacy.

Five

PARADES AND
ENTERTAINMENT

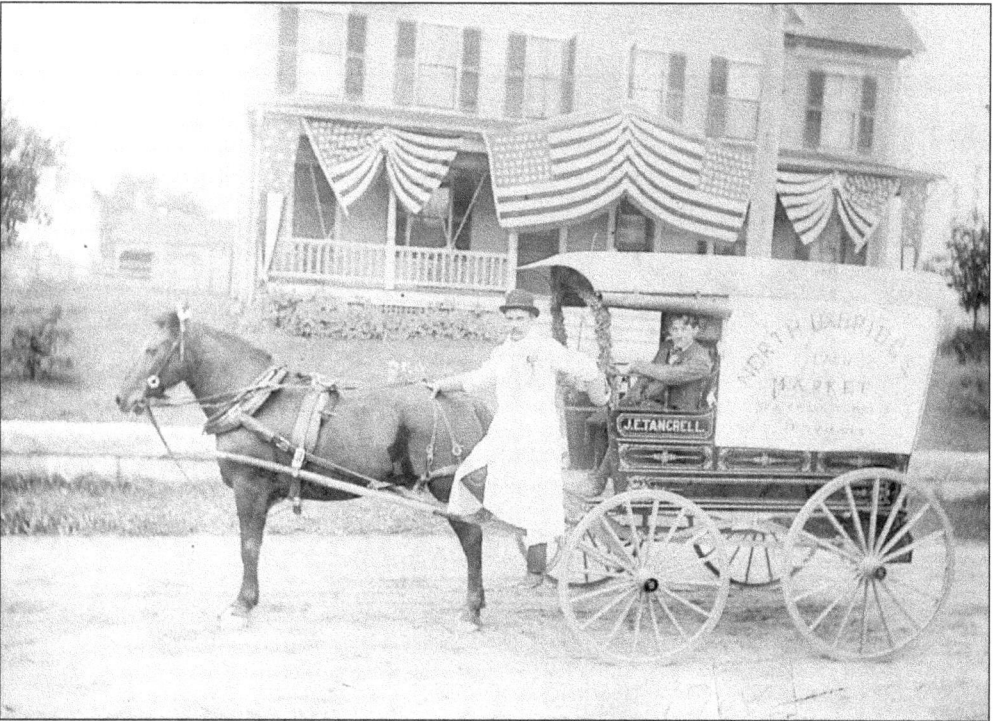

James Tancrell takes part in the 1927 bicentennial parade on his North Uxbridge Market delivery wagon.

These young people dressed in Colonial attire and carrying a model of the Macomber Academy are among those marching in the parade.

Members of the Improved Order of Red Men, dressed in Native American style, relax while waiting to take their place in the parade.

This is the parade entry of the Central Woolen and Stanley Woolen Company.

This WW I army truck and cannon are among the many floats participating in the parade.

The *Santa Maria* and its crew sail smoothly along the parade route.

Uxbridge Worsted Inc. entered this excellent replica of the yarn industry.

Robert Taft and his five sons, Thomas, Robert Jr., Joseph, Daniel, and Benjamin Taft ride proudly in their horse-drawn wagon.

Representatives of St. Mary's Church join the parade in this patriotic entry.

The Ancient Order of United Workmen of Massachusetts is among the many participants.

The Deborah Wheelock Chapter, Daughters of the American Revolution, is represented on this truck, complete with spinning wheel and hand loom.

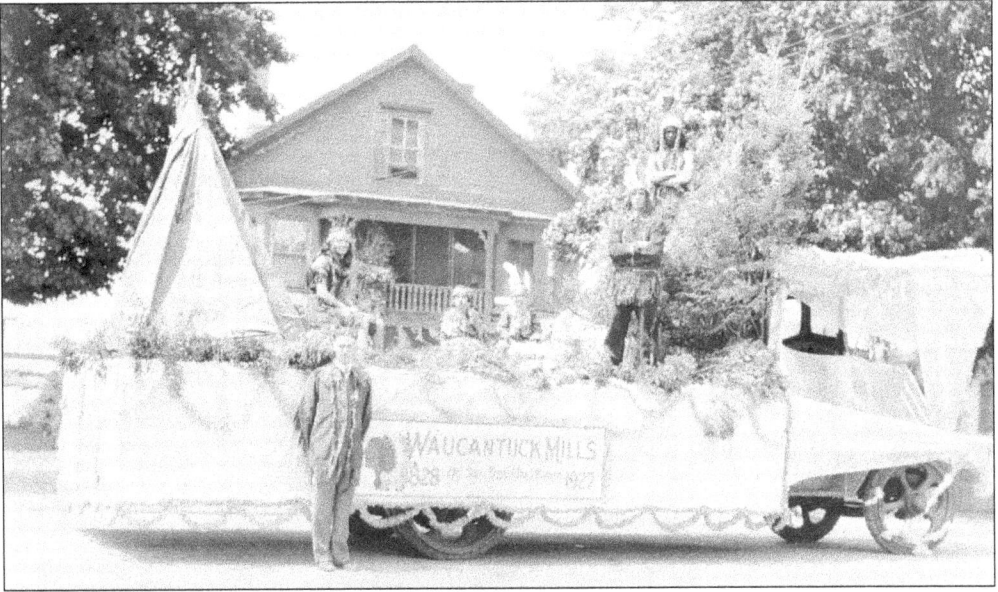

The Waucantuck Mills is another of the many participants in the bicentennial parade. For its entry the company chose an Indian theme, complete with tepee.

Members of the Polish American Club dressed in native costume are, from left to right, as follows: (front row) Anna Jasikouski, Stacia Lemanski, Jennie Novack, Mary Novack, Stella Gniadek, and Josephine Galas; (middle row) Helen Burnat, John Rozak, Anthony Malicz, Stanley Lemick, Stanley Kosciak, Andrew Kosciak, and Anna Myka; (back row) Stefan Augusciak, John Novack, and Stanley Lemanski.

Members of the C.T.A. who participated in a May basket party on May 21, 1917 were, from left to right, as follows: (front row) Maidie Kennedy, Lena Kennedy, Pearl Casey, Anna Murphy, Florence Creighton, Lucille Cook, and Mildred Creighton; (back row) Katie Barker, Mary Clarke, Mae O'Donnell, Mrs. Paul, Marion Tracy, Mabel Laughlin, and Marie Carmody.

The handkerchief shop that was once located in the Capron building, now owned by Charles Lynch, entered this float in the 1927 bicentennial parade. The shop was operated by John Bray and was later housed in the big block on Park Street.

84

Dr. A.E. Gray's children and their friends pose for a picture in this antique wagon, c. 1900.

A production of *Little Almond Eyes* was presented c. 1916 in upper town hall. Participating were, from left to right, as follows: (first row) Glenda Gove, Gladys Gove, Gladys Hudson, Myrtle Hawley, Winnifred Stacey, Lora Morin, Millicent Hudson, Rose Morin, Charlotte Ellsworth, Maitland Bane, Doris Scribner, Grace Blanchard, and unidentified; (second row) Dorothy Gunn, Gertrude Angell, Edna Ehrcke, Helen Sweet, Ruth Chase, Clara Gunn (Little Almond Eyes), Carlton Blanchard, Phyllis Christopher, Abbie Scribner, Mildred Taft, Adwilda Morin, Sadie Anderson, and Harvey Newell; (third row) Grace Gunn, unidentified, Ethel Robins, unidentified, Edith Anderson, unidentified, unidentified, Albert Donald, Clifford Hudson, Celia Kenney, unidentified, and unidentified; (fourth row) unidentified, unidentified, Hazel Anderson, Hazel Judkins, Harold Coombs, Roy Anderson, Howard Holbrook, unidentified, Ernest Wood, unidentified, Louise Ramsey, Winnifred Holbrook, unidentified, and unidentified; (fifth row) Wade Phoenix, unidentified, Oscar Sands, unidentified, Howard Ramsey, George Gunn, and unidentified.

The Tourists Society was formed in 1882. Pictured here, from left to right, are the following: (first row) Hattie Whitmore, Rena Bates, and Alice Slater; (second row) Stella Clarke, Abbie Day, Mary Seagrave, Mrs. D. Wilcox, and Imogene Mascroft; (third row) Emma Newell, Mrs. Lackey, Lila Rawson, Sarah Taft, and Ella Seagrave; (fourth row) Mrs. Johnson, Mrs. Bates, Gertie Legg, Miss Robbins, Mrs. Green, and Mrs. Henry Farnum.

Local town officials and dignitaries marching in the Liberty Bond Parade in 1918 round the corner on Capron Hill (Mendon Street).

Spirit of '76

A fife and drum corps participates in the 1918 Liberty Loan Parade along Mendon Street.

The Uxbridge Grange float is one of many that entered the parade.

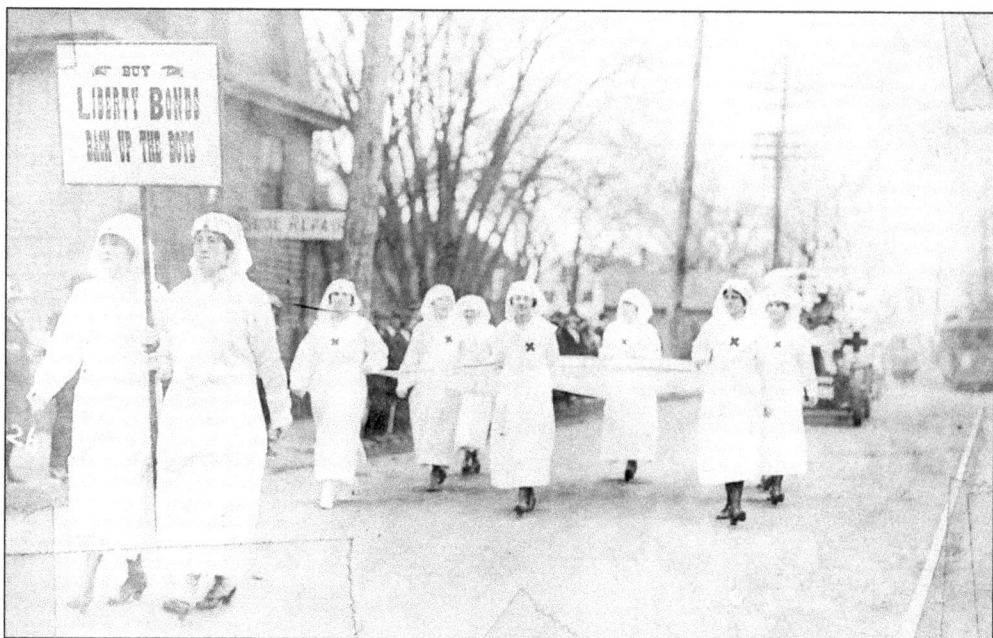

Red Cross nurses take part in the Liberty Loan Parade.

Charles A. Root supported the Liberty Loan Parade by sponsoring the Camp Devens Band. This band was very popular during its time.

Liberty Loan Parade April 20, 1918

This unit of soldiers from Camp Devens accompanied the band and joined the parade marchers.

The Ladies Aid of the Father Matt's Temperance Society poses on the lawn of the Israel Southwick home during the parade.

The Civil War monument on the town common was dedicated on September 14, 1898. More than 3,000 people attended the ceremonies.

The center of town is heavily decorated for Old Home Week in 1908.

The Loyalty Circle, C of F entered this float in the Old Home Week parade, held on September 20, 1908. The float was decorated in purple and white and carried 12 women.

Waiting on Douglas Street for the parade to start is one of many entries in the parade: the Tourist Society's float, a boat on wheels filled with members all dressed in white.

The float entered by the Daughters of the American Revolution was said to be the most unique in the parade. It was drawn by a pair of oxen driven by Rueben Green, left, dressed in Continental costume. The float was decorated in blue and gold and carried ten women in old-time costumes.

Orian Chapter No. 110 Order of the Eastern Star entered a float, decorated in blue and white, that carried a lodge meeting in progress, with the officers at their stations.

The float entered by the Solomon Temple A.F. & A.M., Masons, was done in pink and white and carried a lodge meeting in progress, with officers at their stations.

The Uxbridge Grange float, representing a harvest scene, was the largest in the parade.

In a carriage decorated in red, white, and blue and drawn by two horses, the Women's Relief Corps waits for the parade to commence. The driver is dressed as Uncle Sam.

Joining in the parade is the Waucantuck Mills and C.A. Root entry, which carries a canoe with two Indians.

George Z. Taft, seated on a buckboard with three beagle dogs, takes part in the Old Home Week parade.

The stagecoach carrying the governor and other dignitaries stops at the Hotel Windsor so that they can view the parade from the porch.

Riding in a well-decorated carriage, Gus Seagrave and his daughter pause for a moment on Mendon Street. In the background are C.C. Capron's barn and one of the tenement houses located on Capron Hill.

Six

CHURCHES AND SCHOOLS

The Catholic population of North Uxbridge and Linwood, composed largely of people of French-Canadian descent, had grown so rapidly that the parish of the Good Shepherd was established in that area on October 19, 1904. Until July 1907, Masses were held in the Uxbridge and Northbridge Electric Company building on Maple Street. The Good Shepherd School, built in the rear of the church, opened on June 25, 1922. Reverend Gideon Fontaine was the founder.

In 1770, in consideration of 6 pounds, two parcels of land—one for a burial ground and one for the house of worship—were bought of Moses Farnum. In May 1771, the Quaker Meeting House was completed. Services were held through 1920, when the church as such ceased to exist. At present the doors are opened for Thanksgiving Union services, Quaker services one Sunday a month, weddings on request, and society meetings on request.

The heirs of Alden Homans donated this rare ox brake to the Quaker Meeting House Association. The structure and its contents were moved a distance of 4 miles, from the old Thompson Farm on Chocolog Road to the meetinghouse.

In 1831, a problem arose in the First Congregational Society. Known as the Unitarian Controversy, the problem involved the settlement of a pastor. The more conservative party withdrew from the society, formed the new First Evangelical Congregational Society, and built this new church on the west side of the town common in 1833. The church had several carriage sheds in the rear of the building, a necessity of the time.

The First Congregational Society (Unitarian) built this meetinghouse in 1834 after separating from the old society. The land was purchased from the Capron family and is on the east side of the common. Both the interior and the exterior of the building have been remodeled several times. The town clock, donated in 1869 by Willard Judson, is located in the belfry, where it can be seen by all.

99

The North Uxbridge Baptist Church was organized on January 22, 1842. Services were held in a hall built by Robert Rogerson until the edifice was dedicated on August 4, 1881. Richard Sayles was a large contributor to the cost of the church, located at the corner of North Main and East Hartford Avenue. Extensive repair was necessary after the 1938 hurricane.

In 1852, Reverend Charles O'Reilly purchased land and laid the foundation for St. Mary's Church, a simple wood structure crowning the hill on North Main Street. The "Old Church," as this original St. Mary's parish is referred to, was dedicated in August 1855. Reverend Peter Blinkinsop of Holy Cross College said the Mass and Father Mullady, also of Holy Cross, preached the sermon. Thomas Grimes, E.J. Kelley, and James Daley were the altar boys.

This photograph shows the entrance to St. Mary's Cemetery on Granite Street.

Every year on the Sunday closest to All Saints' Day, the Rev. Richard Murphy led the parishioners through St. Mary's Cemetery, reciting the rosary for the faithful departed.

On March 4, 1923, Reverend Denis P. Sullivan purchased from Charles Whitney the so-called Daniel Taft property on Mendon Street. The property included an impressive house with sufficient land to build a church. The house became the present rectory and, with proper ceremony, ground was broken on the adjoining land for a new St. Mary's Church. On January 31, 1926, Father Sullivan said the first Mass in the new building.

In 1879, a group of Christian people gathered at the house of Mr. E.J. Talbot and formed what is now known as the Taft Memorial United Methodist Church. The meetings were first held in Taft's Hall. The present house of worship was built on part of the old Uxbridge Burying Ground. The completed structure was dedicated in 1880.

In 1895, Jonathan Farnum sold to the town a large piece of land on Mendon Street to be used as a cemetery. The bodies buried in the old cemetery in the center were removed and reburied in this new cemetery, called the Prospect Hill Cemetery. The family of Cornet John Farnum claimed his body as well as the body of his wife, Abigail Farnum, and reburied them in a family plot in the Friends Cemetery on Quaker Highway.

The interior of the Church of the Good Shepherd as it looked originally was quite impressive, with its arched ceiling and a statue of the Good Shepherd high in the middle of the altar.

The last of the one-room schoolhouses to be closed was the Ironstone School. It now belongs to the South Uxbridge Community Association and is used for meetings and other functions of the society. It has been well preserved, and recently a replica of the outhouse was placed on the site.

One of the early one-room schoolhouses, this building was originally the Happy Hollow School. It was removed from its location on Mill Street to Carney Street, where the Boy Scouts used it for their meetings.

The Center School was erected in 1867. In the early years, this school was used as both a high school and an elementary school. It was built on the site of the old Burying Ground on South Main Street. After the high school was built, the Center School held grades one through eight. It continued in operation until 1954, when it was sold and demolished to make way for a new post office. The outhouse at the rear of the building can be seen on the left in this photograph.

After many debates over its location, the first high school building was erected on a lot purchased from C.C. Capron on Mendon Street. In 1937, a new high school was built on Capron Street and this building was used as a junior high school. Later, it was sold to the Catholic church to be used as a social center. It was finally demolished to make way for a parking area for the church.

In 1900, the small one-room schoolhouse near Rogerson's Village was moved to a location near the Crown and Eagle Mill. A large addition was built at a cost of $16,000. This school serviced heavily populated North Uxbridge and is still located on East Hartford Avenue. Classes for kindergarten through eighth grade were held here.

Due to overcrowding in the high school, a new school was built in 1937 on Capron Street. This school is still in service, although much interior and exterior remodeling has been necessary over the years to accommodate the increasing number of students.

106

Completed in 1869, the Center School looked like this before a large addition markedly changed its appearance in 1912. Included in the picture is John W. Wims, who was born on September 13, 1857, according to town records. This fact would date the picture as between 1869 and 1875. The bearded gentleman in front of the pupils may have been J. Mason Macomber, prefect of Uxbridge Academy from 1840 to 1850.

This is a rare picture of longtime third-grade teacher Minnie Clark, who stands in the third row at the left with her class at the Center School. The photograph was taken in 1906.

Here is a rare picture of Minnie Clark, long time third grade teacher at center school. Girl in middle of second row

This is teacher Mary Dunleavy's second grade at the Center School *c.* 1909. Pictured, from left to right, are the following: (first row) James Carmody, Bill Deorsey, Ernest Henry, Lester Vayo, Charlie Barton, Pat Lizotte, Leo Brady, ? Waterhouse, two unidentified boys, Byron Taft, and William Cloutier; (middle row) Bessie Reynolds, Annette Laroque, unidentified, Alice Shaughnessy, three unidentified girls, Edith Goldthwaite, Myrtice Taft, unidentified, Gladys Gove, Blanche Montville, and Margaret Landry; (back row) unidentified, Joe Montville, ? Horton, Joe Goddard, two unidentified pupils, Punk Wheeler, unidentified, ? Goddard, two unidentified girls, Agnes Shean, and Dot Hudson.

This class picture at North Uxbridge School has only one identified student: Romeo Gervais, back row, fourth from the left.

This is an early picture of a class at the Wheelocksville School. Neither the pupils nor the teacher have been identified.

Shown in this class picture at the Wheelocksville School are, from left to right, the following: (front row)teacher Harriet Aldrich, Katie Nulty, Agnes Dowling, ? Hartshorn, Fred Dowling, John Nulty, Willie Vayo, Kate Sessions, and Sylvia Vayo; (middle row) Michael Brady, Charles Riley, James Bresnahan, Charles Henry, William Reynolds, George E. Willard, Pearl Whitaker, Julia Dowling, Patsy Carmody, Meritt Wood, Susie Willard, and Darius Henry; (back row) Jennie Wheelock, ? Reynolds, Hannah Kennedy, John Conway, Sarah Garside, Maggie Willard, Kate Bresnahan, Kate Roach, and Mary Conway.

These women taught at the North Uxbridge School in 1921. They are Elizabeth Conway, grades seven and eight; Mary Roche, grade six; Helen Healy, grade five; Corrine Taft, grade four; Lena Kennedy, grade three; Annie Daley, grade two; Blanche McKendy, grade one-A; and Sarah Garrity, grade one-B.

Members of the fifth grade at the Center School in 1912 are, from left to right, as follows: (first row) Fred Gendron, Thomas Rice, Roy Kerns, Kenneth Henry Hudson, Edward Murphy, Martin Esten, Lawrence Gadbois, and Henry Landry; (second row) Alfred Esten, Edward Garrity, Gladys Horton, Ethel Ballou, Edward Reiley, Marion Gove, Louis Brady, and James Devlin; (third row) Edward Wesgan, Howard Donald, May Whitten, Dorothy Gunn, Katherin Carmody, Mary Barr, Amelia Burt, and Bernadette Dorsey; (fourth row) Hellen Anderson, Ella Leonard, Dorothy McCaffrey, Samuel Richardson, Edwin Newell, Sylvester Thomas, and Joseph Lizotte.

Teacher Mrs. Mulligan stands with her students at the Ironstone Schoolhouse in 1939. Seated are, from left to right, the following: (first row) Joey Knapik, Pearl Appleoff, and Peggy Thornton; (second row) Donald LeClaire, Eleanor Appleoff, and Bobby Platt; (third row) Jane Kollett and Gordon Kollett; (fourth row) Shirley Frisk, Jeannette Tubias, and John Adams; (fifth row) Muriel LeClerc, Lillian Kollett, and Harriet Appleoff.

On the Uxbridge High School basketball team in 1925–1926 were, from left to right, the following: (front row) Rykoski, Chaffee, team captain Hauge, Carroll, and Atamian; (back row) team manager Harold Aldrich, Perry, Andrews, Tancrell, and coach Francis J. Splaine.

Joe Brannigan, mgr

Manager Joe Brannigan (correctly spelled Branigan) was with the 1914–1915 Uxbridge High crack basketball quintet, which the *Boston Globe* picked as one of the five best teams in the state.

Two members of the 1914–1915 Uxbridge High crack basketball quintet are Ernie Wood, left, and George "Gubby" McDermott, right.

Ernie Wood.

Geo. Gubby McDermott

The 1914–1915 Uxbridge High crack basketball quintet also included Mert Pennell, upper left, Al "Tot" Tracy, upper right, and Hubbie Cook, lower right.

A group of high school students gathers on the steps of the school c. 1907–1908.

This photograph shows the Uxbridge High School Class of 1912 on the steps of the Treasury Building in Washington, D.C., on March 26, 1912.

Members of the Uxbridge High School Class of 1913 and guests pose for a photograph on the lawn at Mount Vernon.

Members of the Class of 1922 pose on the steps of the high school. In the picture are, from left to right, the following: (first row) Helen Fiske, Mary Kennedy, Shirley Gove, Marion Wilson, Helen Keough, Noreen Brick, Harriet Aldrich, and Carrie Ferris; (second row) Esther Moorehouse, May Andrews, Loretta Girard, Mary Malley, Katherine Parnell, and Dorothy Chaffee; (third row) Ambrose Carroll, Chester Kiernan, Earl Aldrich, Leon "Pat" Blaine, Harry Atamian, and Leo "Pete" Lynch; (fourth row) Paul Roche, John McCollum, Russell Blanchard, and John Collins.

The students of Uxbridge High School gather on the lawn in front of the school for this group

The Uxbridge High School Class of 1945 performed many services for the town during World War II. Class members assisted town officers with the rationing program, joined the Crop Corps to dig potatoes in Maine, served as official aircraft observers for the Aircraft Warning Service

picture in 1921.

CLASS OF 1925

PHOTO BY BOWARAM

at the observation post on Hazel Street, worked at the ARP Telephone Service at Legion Headquarters on Douglas Street, and took part in the scrap metal drive. Many class members had assumed "the duties of manhood" before graduation and were absent from the photograph.

117

Helen Ryan, shown standing behind the drum, formed the Uxbridge High School Band in the late 1920s. This picture of the band was taken in front of the high school.

Seven

DISASTERS

In 1927, the West River overflowed. This picture of the Waucantuck Mill shows the flooded area in back of the building.

In 1896, a fire broke out in the Gunn Block and quickly spread to the Taft Building. It started around midnight and continued throughout the night. Help was sent from Worcester, but the blaze raged out of control until 4:15 a.m.

The flames from the Gunn Block leapt across the street and ignited the Gredig Block. The fire destroyed the Goldthwaite Block and the Macomber Building. The Whitmore Block and the Hotel Windsor were unharmed.

The Blackstone National Bank had quarters in the south end of the Taft Block, but all the cash and valuable documents were in the vault. Many books and papers were burned. Paper money was partially burned but was replaced by the federal government. The bank reopened in the Harris Block.

In 1906, the center of town was again the scene of a great fire. Christian Gredig's building burned to the ground. The fire destroyed S.B. Taft's block and the Goldthwaite Block. Gredig at once began laying plans for a new two-story brick building. Taft also rebuilt with brick. The Goldthwaite Block was not rebuilt. The two new brick buildings still stand today.

A flood hit Uxbridge in 1927. This photograph shows the waters of the Mumford River threatening the bridge on Mendon Street near Lynch's drugstore.

Drabbletail Brook drained Shuttle Shop Pond, running underground across Main Street to empty into the Mumford River. In the flood of 1927, lower left, the brook's usual channel filled and the water came over the top, flooding the town center. The picture at the lower right shows the floodwater from Drabbletail Brook rushing under the railroad bridge on Mendon Street.

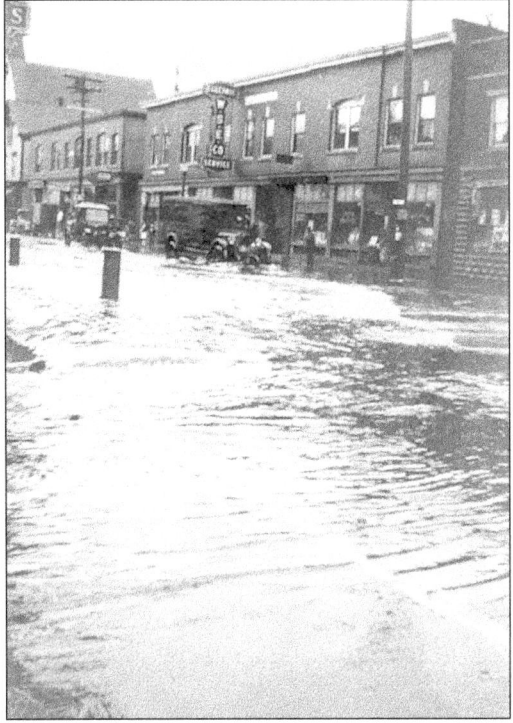

Looking west toward the town center, upper left, the floodwaters nearly cover the fire hydrant on Mendon Street. Looking south in the center, upper right, the rushing water creates waves as Drabbletail Brook continues to surge toward the Mumford River.

On September 23, 1938, Uxbridge was hit by a strong hurricane. Winds over 100 miles an hour roared through the town. In the center, the roof of the Taft Block was torn off and deposited on Mendon Street. The tower of the town hall crumbled. Church steeples were toppled, and many trees were uprooted.

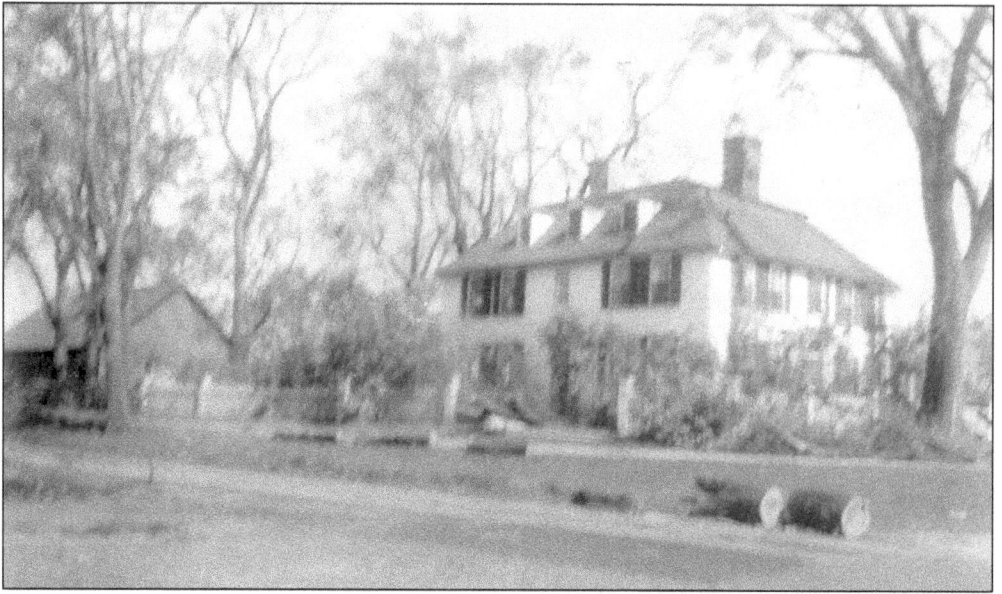

This huge tree in front of the Bazeley home on South Main Street was uprooted. No damage was done to the house but the road was blocked until the tree was removed.

In 1955, Hurricane Edna visited Uxbridge and once more the high winds toppled huge trees. This scene on Hazel Street shows the hurricane's power.

Hurricane Edna broke this tree off at its base in front of the library.

Throughout the town huge trees lay on the ground, felled by hurricane winds.

This picture of the library was taken after the blizzard of February 6, 1978, which left behind snowdrifts more than 5 feet tall.

Throughout the town snow from the blizzard of 1978 buried cars, such as this one in front of Village Motor Sales on North Main Street.

In 1991, a tragic fire occurred in North Uxbridge. The James Whitin estate, known as Gray Rock, burned. The house was unoccupied at the time of the fire. Flames roared through the main building, shadowing the front portico. The large stable in the rear was destroyed as well.

Rubble was all that remained of the beautiful home built by James Whitin so many years ago. Today, it has all been cleared away and only memories remain.

Water from the swollen West River rushes through the Waucantuck Mill during the flood of November 4, 1927. So much of history is carried away by disasters such as these.

www.ingramcontent.com/pod-product-compliance
Lightning Source LLC
Chambersburg PA
CBHW080910100426

42812CB00007B/2231